THE OWL
WAS A
BAKER'S
DAUGHTER

THE COLORADO PRIZE FOR POETRY

Strike Anywhere, by Dean Young
selected by Charles Simic, 1995

Summer Mystagogia, by Bruce Beasley
selected by Charles Wright, 1996

The Thicket Daybreak,
by Catherine Webster
selected by Jane Miller, 1997

Palma Cathedral, by Michael White
selected by Mark Strand, 1998

Popular Music, by Stephen Burt
selected by Jorie Graham, 1999

Design, by Sally Keith
selected by Allen Grossman, 2000

A Summer Evening, by Geoffrey Nutter
selected by Jorie Graham, 2001

Chemical Wedding, by Robyn Ewing
selected by Fanny Howe, 2002

Goldbeater's Skin, by G. C. Waldrep
selected by Donald Revell, 2003

Whethering, by Rusty Morrison
selected by Forrest Gander, 2004

Frayed escort, by Karen Garthe
selected by Cal Bedient, 2005

Carrier Wave, by Jaswinder Bolina
selected by Lyn Hejinian, 2006

Brenda Is in the Room and Other Poems,
by Craig Morgan Teicher
selected by Paul Hoover, 2007

One Sun Storm, by Endi Bogue Hartigan
selected by Martha Ronk, 2008

The Lesser Fields, by Rob Schlegel
selected by James Longenbach, 2009

Annulments, by Zach Savich
selected by Donald Revell, 2010

Scared Text, by Eric Baus
selected by Cole Swensen, 2011

Family System, by Jack Christian
selected by Elizabeth Willis, 2012

Intimacy, by Catherine Imbriglio
selected by Stephen Burt, 2013

Supplice, by T. Zachary Cotler
selected by Claudia Keelan, 2014

The Business, by Stephanie Lenox
selected by Laura Kasischke, 2015

Exit Theater, by Mike Lala
selected by Tyrone Williams, 2016

Instead of Dying, by Lauren Haldeman
selected by Susan Howe, 2017

The Owl Was a Baker's Daughter,
by Gillian Cummings
selected by John Yau, 2018

THE OWL WAS A BAKER'S DAUGHTER

Gillian Cummings

POEMS

The Center for Literary Publishing
Colorado State University

For information about permission to reproduce
selections from this book, write to
The Center for Literary Publishing
attn: Permissions
9105 Campus Delivery
Colorado State University
Fort Collins, Colorado 80523-9105.

Printed in the United States of America.

Library of Congress Cataloging-in-Publication Data
Names: Cummings, Gillian (Poet), author.
Title: The owl was a baker's daughter / Gillian Cummings.
Description: Fort Collins, Colorado : The Center for Literary Publishing,
    Colorado State University, [2018] | Includes bibliographical references. |
    Colorado Prize for Poetry, 2018
Identifiers: LCCN 2018031541 (print) | LCCN 2018032525 (ebook) | ISBN
    9781885635662 (electronic) | ISBN 9781885635655 (pbk. : alk. paper)
Subjects: | LCGFT: Prose poems.
Classification: LCC PS3603.U65556 (ebook) | LCC PS3603.U65556 A6 2018 (print)
    | DDC 811/.6--dc23
LC record available at https://lccn.loc.gov/2018031541

The paper used in this book meets the minimum requirements of the
American National Standard for Information Sciences-Permanence of Paper
for Printed Library Materials, ANSI Z39.48-1984.

1 2 3 4 5   22 21 20 19 18

for Susan and Roger
in memory

and for my late Zen teacher Susan Jion Postal
and my late therapist Dr. David F. Pelino:
may there be something that saves all beings
the way your kindness saved me

Ophelia.
"They say the owl was a baker's daughter. Lord, we know what we are, but we know not what we may be. God be at your table!"

—William Shakespeare, *Hamlet,*
Act IV, Scene V

CONTENTS

II.

A Note from the Final Judge

Gillian Cummings writes:

> You have been many people
> but none of them is you.

In a letter John Keats sent to Richard Woodhouse, dated October 27, 1818, he wrote: "(. . . I am a Member; that sort distinguished from the wordsworthian or egotistical sublime; which is a thing per se and stands alone) it is not itself—it has no self—it is every thing and nothing—It has no character—it enjoys light and shade; it lives in gusto, be it foul or fair, high or low, rich or poor, mean or elevated . . ."

The singular Gillian Cummings is (as Keats would surely agree) a "camelion Poet" who lives in the sharp, conjuring, mythical, drifting, unexpected, mellifluous music of her poems:

> A bobbin doesn't unspool thread, it winds
> twigs into her hazard of hair, a lair for
> empty breezes and the promise of elsewhere.

Cummings's "elsewhere" is "only a matter / of something asking to be let in."

Dear Reader, I implore you: Read these poems. Listen to their music. Proceed at your own risk.

—JOHN YAU

I

All of It Alive

Meanwhile, she wants to die and does
not know: to the body and its burden
or to the self that pretends to be body.
She steps and one thousand moths lift,
lift lightly, spiral-whirl. They flicker and fleck,
weaving a world around her. Over roots
impossibly stone-clung, moss-covered,
the river plumbs the places where it pools.
Some bubbles, in eddies, last longer,
lingering in the swirl. As moths
cross over, one by one, she goes under,
under, the place where water
doesn't foam. This fleeting world—
achingly, without her—
all of it alive.

Of the Notebook's Eyes

Try to not exist, says the gypsy, weaving
white through wind. Red clover. Timid
fleabanes, too scared to widen beyond
their small, spiked circles. A doe and fawn
sauntering through a field of loosestrife, lost
to sky's names. *Can you be in the ten thousand
things and not be?* says the granite grown
mossy, licheny, over the stream swirling
into shapes she scribbles in the asylum.
She draws to keep the window closed.
Yet open. She lives to learn no window,
no room, no door. She lives to learn nothing.
And yet clover. And yet loosestrife. And yet foam.

Of Water and Echo

She is in the tree by the river
that sings in the tree, in the mouth
of the tree waxing mournful on water.
The hively shrilling of bees, darker
than honey, more homely than resinous gold.
It's cold and damp in the song of water
ringing of ripple, of rapid and fade, of
day's end and the coming of blade, of the axe's
edge opening the throat of bold call. Of
what the moon won't say in any emergency,
any anxious fall, reds in the greens of summer,
the lone hollow of tree by the river
in which she sings, water in her teeth.

Moon-Girls of the Burning Barn, 1

No trinket, no bauble, no bell
luring them out of their lair safely to home.
Outside the narrow gate, no lollipop, no
ostrich. They know in this light
trees have auras like squid, secrets taste
like a railroad's wish to lead nowhere
and its station rides home with tiny horses.
The tired stalls' snow-smudge of desire.
Golds, golds, red, red—color shreds fall
even in this log-laid hall of buried banter:
they breathe its smoke-braids and want to
weave through their hair witch-hazel,
wintergreen, whitethorn berries.

Moon-Girls of the Burning Barn, 2

They're afraid of the hunter's moon,
its over-bite on the dark bread of memory,
how love is what leaves do to flame. Here
a baked apple's bitter and the barn holds
buckets in its oven, no crisped raisins, no
cinnamon sprinkle, no maple poured. So
Littlest asks, *Do you want to play beast with me?*
and Oldest bests, *I am sleeping like a babe
under a hatchet,* doesn't guess hell, says
of the dead, *They go,* no release in these skies
for the loneliest bird—until Penitent begs,
Pretty-please for a merry-go-round tiny horses can ride.
And the moon-pearl pulls them wayward.

Of Blossoms and Ghosts

The trees looked wistful today.
Were they missing their lost limbs?
In the duck and quail of dusk,
lost is a word of houses, as in
The map follows the road that once led
to this charred, red door of be gone.
The trees said it gently, like *bygone,*
looked to the lake water for what
the water saw. But the water coaxed,
What breathes and sees the broadest spaces?
How much light does a tree take into a bud?
Is it possible to love like that,
like timid tucks of fabric unable
to unfold, yet unfolding?

Low to Ground and Listening

Is vinca less vinca because it's
called vinca? Or onion grass more onion
when a child pulls bulbs from stringy soil?
Is a heart more heart in moments she feels
its beating? Blood in her purples, in the stink
on the skinny girl's hands, the brushed dirt—
she flirts with a fear of this season. It's a closet
opening when she was caught in winter's
last coat, boots that treaded gravel to graven
God's image of better Earths after, a pure
purpose for pebbles and woe. Snow was familiar
and foreign as her own echo, asking, asking,
Are they the same? The desire to end a life
and the need to know how: a flower's simple bliss?

Here the Woods Come in Too Close

A flock of birds crowds a crust of bread.
Maples all-fall-down now, but here or there
a last rose, last blood drop to stain fabric.
See? Each stitch builds a birch or the throat of an oak:
some things only speak sorrow by being pierced through.
A tunnel is too fragile a place to hear peace speak,
especially for a swivel-girl who knows only
trouble, how it turns, turns like the game
of dimes or dreidels, disappears as God
calling berries but bittersweet, touched:
Talk to me, doppelgänger, doll rolled in flour or ash.

Of Bubbles and Milk

The littlenesses start littling in pink,
white, yellow. She knows dandelion,
the weed one, the one not supposed to be,
as she is not. Exit. Thinks she's a nest,
but the egg followed a robin to another home.
A bobbin doesn't unspool thread, it winds
twigs into her hazard of hair, a lair for
empty breezes and the promise of elsewhere.
The littlenesses might taste like soap
bubbles and milk, ashes and snow, if only
ibises and ostriches lived in her wild, not
on wallpaper's fast-fading landscape.
To her, the lure of God is a raindrop
fallen on a flock of banking starlings.

Flowers for the Executioner

To God, her heart isn't good—
she wants morning glories wilting
on wire fences, a furrow of weeping blues.
Then branches of bittersweet betokening winter.
Love your enemies, bless them that curse you.
She covets the forest its feather-like
fringes, its owl-blooms to nighten her hair.
Do good to them that hate you. Coaxes marigolds
to close their copper pages in soil's frosted
herbarium, where dreams sleep, rooting earth
with the breath of extinguishing stars.

A Matryoshka Doll Is a Nest Made of Eggs

At least she is safe. At least
her body. And if she breaks, as she
must, if she splits or shatters or goes
fine, at least she grows smaller
and smaller with each dose
of another's pleasure, as sparrows
narrow their numbed bodies to burrow
into holes carved from cold. And if she is
all hole, opening always as sky
opens to take in the wound of snow,
at least she holds, at core, a kernel of girl.

Silence, a Prayer of Wax

Cochlea of the mind, poor snail shell.
Consciousness, too slow and hollow
to make the echoes stop. You of nothing,
nowhere-gone, forever going, without cease.
Without cease of slurs, those incidents of insults
that ring scales to the blurred beat of no timpani.
Never but a heat fevering over the hurt, the hurt.
All songs ever smugly sung, sung wrong,
all awry in the testament of your coiled,
tapered tubes—stop now, please, poor mind,
rest, the tired girl wants to go home and light
candles. Let their talking wicks be an almostness.

Little Heavenling

Before bed, she whispers prayers
into an alembic: last thimbleful of snow.
Melted where a dove mourns, blood
off pelt from a stag marooning bent grass.
Wine she wants Jesus not to have chaliced
so no stumble and slur to unbless
the thousandfold names for God.
Cucurbit of night. Cucurbit of piled pillows.
Boil, steam, cool. She wakes to shadows
stalking the promontory where water pries
open the shut eyes of rocks. Whose cloak
billows with such rage of blank sight?
Notice nothing, little heavenling, small hellborn,
notice not how hardness softens by the soft, a rift
mends when what's unwearing fits unworn.

Faint Stars of Dread

Unbearable, the snowdrops, as if winter
could be something lived through.
Overmuch, this reminder of life,
the dead earth candling its sorrows
with bowed heads in silent mourning.
Implausible, to have been—
meaning to have harmed, to have cut
the bud by the root—as if being could ever,
perpetually, end with softness. Or begin
in Kyrie eleison, a call echoed by white bells.

Memory of Sin

What enters, enters of its own.
Frost on the windows, filaments of ice,
the touch of ghosts too timid to enter in.
No bell, no knocker, nothing to announce
the chill, the jolt, the flare of what comes
in the night. What comes, comes like wind.
Shatters the silence and silences the broken,
the pieces of tattle, of complaint. What comes,
comes as echo, the loss, the near world echoing
the loss, of something begun and abandoned:
a sad moon rising faintly over the earth,
shrunk down to a dime, to fit in a pocket.
Then further diminished, or then tossed away.

Unknowing the Clouds

The cloud of forgetting below her,
full of sea-softened, blue bottle shards,
full of hydrangeas and swans and jays
and everything maned—horses a-gallop,
sorrel through sorrel, roan through the moan
of fast winds—she's sore, she's sorrowful, she can't
push them down: thoughts of the earth she loved.
The cloud of unknowing above her—*Pierce it,*
she's told, *with a ray of bare heart, of holy ardor.*
But the horses have hooves to trample her
simple, blue veil. The pieces of beach glass
scratched with memories of cuts—now to forget them.
But she's caught between, she's nowhere, going slow.
She wants God, but more what she means is clean madness.

Unwriting the Sentence

Nightly, it flaps out, flaps out—
not a cry but a quietness, it had become
bigger, empty of starlight. Sleep tucked it
far beneath a bed of wings and smoke-moon,
beneath the room rocking a slow tug
at her boatlessness. It would come for her.
Mornings, she knew this better than curtains
know to keep out light. She once feared
this would be more than she would ever know:
the book of pages left unturned, sullied
with some phantom coffee stains, underlines,
mostly the erasures. It was the erasures.
In the end, it was the erasures
of love that hurt most.

Of the Cloud In-Between

Let it come from the cloud,
her kindness, her cure. Let it cushion
on nothing, or rise, her sore soul, up,
into the realm of bodies like cumulous
blossoms, unbuttoned blooms. Let her hair
billow down, locks like snakes, into light,
into dark, let the swamp, let mud-life,
let serpent-lick sting her back to health,
poison push her through the in-between womb.
It's better, much better, that she should float.
Death is already, anyway, here. Let death.
Let her balance on nothing, a pillow of air.

Song of Languor

She slept lightly there, but meant it—
sparrow, sparrow, linger. She slept lightly there,
then spied them: little blooms of white, little blooms—
Little blooms now fall: forget them. In the undergrowth,
just traces. These last blooms are white, are fleabanes. Tiny
white daisies, called fleabanes, cling to moss on stones,
and breathe streams—streams that she'd forget, once witness,
witness of this white—water's cry. Sad as stones that sink,
in last dreams. Falling through this now, this moment—
no longer this now, this moment—*only a bird, unsheltering love*—
in the trees above, these traces. Now they hurt too much,
these traces. Why are last blooms white, are fleabanes?
They're death's color too, these daisies. It's a last, lost cry—

Death's Secrets like a Box

A box of dried flowers, death's secret:
crab apple crinkles to powder, lavender—
broken—betokens no grace. But her simples
are simple. And the moon's face in water
breaking. And breaking again. Telling a story
of how nothing—ever—stays, even this blank
night with its scald of cold, her blue fingers.
And what would she say, gone beyond
the worst? Every death suffused with neither
a quiet nimbus nor the fog's persistence
on how sight is never clear. She saw. Saw
her mind like ravens over a battlefield.
And that was enough.

II

A toy in blood

If I carry a doll in my womb, if I birth only eyes, blue, if I am this doll
and a key winds me sideways and soft till the tremor of my body forgets
things small and encauled—oh, small and mostly forbidden—do I then
bless with absence my true yearning? Do I grow liltingly in moist places
or should I seek the low tomb of unmown grasses? To die of what you
long for is to be asked a question of silence and to know your answer
howls—but what if I drop this doll and her skull doesn't break, the flower
never droops on its stem?

I shall good lesson keep

Moon-pearls low on meadows do not a summer's shine mean. But sometimes, before silver filigrees flowers in dawn's frost, a blur of mist makes most believable the beauty even of those long blooms of prurient purples shepherds call orchids—or what, I can't say. I look not far in the dark. Nor would I risk but daisies. Tell me, though, if the story is short, a rose of state, how it grows in its hot magentas. Tell, because he gave me this twin bouquet and the twain did droop and dry. I hold them now for perfume but what comes is a scent scant as dew and scalding as moon's quiet.

The steep and thorny way

I mean nothing. I lose my thinking as a cat its ball of yarn. The ball rolls away, downwards, even if no slope to a slippery floor. Downwards, as what is higher has to lower into us. Prayer happens first in heaven and enters us through what—we know water sips us in its self-savoring cold, fast from ice-melt off mountains. I would not wish a thief no less a god the burden of cross or crown of pain, and yet—a castle is doom enough with its tapestried stone. Downwards. There are flames of hellfire enough in a rose. And I thought God liked my modesty.

Vows of heaven

I begin in happenstance. From whence come here and why, into arms that do not hold me, as sky in an egg births a bird and flees—I don't remember my own flight. What blood, what heat seeking sameness. Nests untether moss by twig—lesser whitethroat, dark-eyed junco, linnet, twite—yet heaven finds itself half-hatchling here. I'd not be caught by desire's wound wire, were it not my soul seeking its own death. Something closes, white wings over frail brood—a forgetting of night's shut sky. It should be easy—gray partridge, quail, godwit, cuckoo—to renounce what lunacy craves.

Pale as his shirt

The silk, linen, cotton, the cloth stretched across the hoop. The needle, the needle, prick and blood on a sun-blasted peony of thread. Who is he now that I should fear him so, when I'm a ghost of cloth hunting these rooms, alive only to the door that exits him to sleep? I'm his thorn. Warning of unseemliness, I'm no better than a tattered robe no prince would deign to wear. I shall pull out some of my hair. Less stain of seduce, to appear unwound so.

So piteous and profound

I am not wise but last night saw a field of oxeye daisies, how shy flowers flocked to be the same sheep, lambs of whorled petals ingathering white, that sun in their center like a stamp of all that glows. I skipped the wide lawn of Elsinore in greening summer and did not know love's pain. But how plain to be lowly and among, how givingly and good. Should I not have been released? What breath could shatter man's bulk is only the way a body takes heaven into its bones, takes the wide and welkin, the ever-bright star-glare, the bordering whole . . . Bring him back to me, please.

Perfume lost

First sun. Then wind. Then clouds across the windowed wall. So his love should have been a grace, now doom deepening. No, I must be a silence, crave only God's key. I heard of a girl once killed by a glove, poison in its perfume. Such trinkets—filigree buttons, ruby brooch, lambskin gloves with cuffs of lace—fragranced with civet, musk, or ambergris, to stimulate a stirring? I would not wish it. My prayer once was his fingers in my hair. Matins and vespers. Now, no gold to wear down by the water. I'd wear my gold tiara with gold-threaded robes of black—the water giving me back my inky halo, giving me back my luck.

Could beauty

If he must, he'll break me. I haven't more than brush and powder of modesty and no story of make-up that could hide what love milks mild. A child, a child, hence a woman with no need to whiten with eggshells, lilies, ivory, no need for lips saffroned to shine. He once implied he would have been mine, or rather—look, the pine-tops brush needles through air that could be our hair! Cones for his ringlets! A shame so. A pity. To be two bodies betokened by the borrowed cries of wind, a serendipity of twig tips, unsearching.

Like sweet bells jangled

A bell has a soul. A bell is a bird with a call like thunder or the thin, tingling whisper of snow. Most moments, its clapper hangs in shame of speech, capped in a rigor by darkness that would muffle our God. But what does God hear when belfry bangs out song bad enough to our lowly earth-ears? A soul has a bell. Something of a person to join in joyous ringing. Birds of our throats. We fly, we float, given music. Our voices forget us. They exist whole only in God. *Go*, he told me. Or his soul said, *Go. Home. To the silence. To death's chapel of bells.*

A grass-green turf

Pilgrims, we, if God wrinkles a shell in our shade. They say the sea calls to its missing mollusk in whorls of whelk as if to mourn it. But search the sand—pebbles, not pearl. And fish hear not a pretty. Oh, a whale won't eat an apple, no matter how it's cored! No sea in the season of fruit. Careless, careless, whim-jostled trees! Such softness in orchards allows bees their sting—they wax wanton in their honey—but come appling autumn, what falls only lies, swollen with rain. Did I say whale? Lucky, to carry a prophet inside. He'd speak from my one rib. Build a table and deck it with icon, ivory bowl, candlestick. Trim the wick and light it. Only thus can we smoke the hive. Combed and tallowed. Only thus we burn, remembering.

The owl was a baker's daughter

If earth is oven enough for my father's body, I won't eat a cake that flies. No, no, no—but night hears *Who?* as a question and cherry pies come out feathered in silvers, golds. Brown at the throat where words turned to molten syrup under crust—whose edges? *Who?* Where do we end? Ah, stir us with no spoon but a knife, dirt is all our company. Would I were the moon. Misted over and round as a chipped china plate. It's late to dine but too early for worms, so let me shine eerily upon you. I'll enter the hall quietly slippered, my body gossamered white.

III

A Dream of Sea Urchins

Forever wed to water, you drift far
into ocean. Here, no harebell, no cowslip,
no rosemary nor rue—just seahorses
in the sting of brine and otters
who clutch spiny prey with such
innocence, they mother their meal
with lullaby. Mermaidlike, you cleave
to blue, carve yourself into waves
that wash memory away. Here,
salt tangle of your hair, whale song,
rain's drum, a difference. How
forgetting is one blessing
of death's ongoing everness.

When World Is Whale

Something surfaces. Not an idea. Not
an idea of an idea or even its underside,
though just afterwards, beneath the surface,
a white-green shadow, or the opposite of shadow,
fades into darker depths below. You know nothing,
not where it came from, not why it appears
or shows a largeness built from a myriad
of smallnesses so little they pretend not to be,
before they are caught, caught by the one, this one,
this presence of something, someone, moving
below the motion of all you can't see, all you have
forgotten in the sleep of your sleep, cradle-rocked
above what you would call love: of water for air, of
inside for outside, of black for the blue it breathes.

Moon-Girls of the Medicine

You were about to float away
so they taught you not to. Softly
into quiet they come, finely, into
spooked light—winged ones they bring,
goldfinch, marlin, wren in enormous
nest: the *begin again,* spring to startle
your winter out of sleep's *either you'll wake*
to wind that washes you like song or you'll open
eyes on sky untrumpeted in old tempests of stars;
either you'll come back to your body or you won't.
But the girls hover over you with their grass-
messes of hair, their eyes mercy-mild, and what
the birds teach in such communal twig-
tangle is simple: *how alone, we break;*
how we're saved by one another.

To Limn a Limbed Thing

In this life, save the body,
which is the fruit of many lives.
Espaliered pear: how heaviness
lavishes the twisted boughs with
sugary sustenance tamed taut
in gnarl and gold. You would hold this
autumn's omen, press to chest a prayer:
that your life become bounteous, useful
as a gathering of pears dappled red.
Awaited, the gift of bindings, of trellised,
forced growth. Accustomed, the swept
azure. Why mourn sheltering shade?
God swoops like taloned rain.
God a bird in your branches.

They Break Open in Sun but Stay Dark

You have been many people
but none of them is you. You live
in a place of dogwood petals fallen
on lake water. You live in a place of sleep.
You don't call the petals bracts, or the white-
tipped garlic mustard weeds, or the bees busybodies
built of honey where they plumb the plump, far-
flung centuries of peonies. You say all these are
the hollows brightness makes once the bones
of sorrow won't speak. Or break. Or sift the book
of wind into ashes. You once heard of God
and thought, *Oh, but to name a thing power cuts
humility into thousands of signatures writ on leaves
that just want to stay leaves.* And you have been a leaf.

Portrait of a Storm

Anyone could have seen the result,
the gaping gash in ground. How the tree
wanted that fast love so fiercely, nothing
and no one could have fixed it from falling.
So you had seen: how the tree breathed
with the vigor of wind. Was it just a habit
of mind, the loose, then taut, thread-pulls
of thought? What is it to say a tree? The wind?
You'd make it yours, stillness swaying into
deeper stillness. You'd hold it if you could,
cradle the dusk, clasp tight what passed as beauty.
The speech of rain: it was only a matter
of something asking to be let in.

Of Thread and Absence

Dusk equals a quilted, seamed-through sky,
hydrangea petals purple, hydrangea petals blue,
stitched with wobble and bite. But tread softly,
needle of moon-shoes, tread and thread what we
would call a little today into a gianter tomorrow.
Oh, pink and pink and gone, and the goneness
a thorough going, where we would venture when
rocks turn rabbits and sight enters the hole of its
mote, gone, gone bone, gone home of the prayer-
hidden, hallelujah-heavy heaven that cried (and for us).

Of the Light Before Darkness

At dusk, we have a hope,
a famine we feign would be
plenty. The air doesn't lift us
to the tops of the copper beeches.
The air wants, *Wider, wider.*
We open our arms
to a number that subtracts
what we hold from the zero
that binds us blind to bliss.

When the Shepherd Sleeps

Sheep, sheep, O unreason, you huddle
in muck and muddle of the pasture, pulling
the last grass left. Cold, under russeted oaks
and autumn's bare birches, under nubby,
thin coat of too-soon sheared fleece, neither
impatient nor angered by limp leg or hoof rot,
you nestle together as rain begins, a drizzle
mustering to downpour, and the youngest
among you never bleats but bears a small bell's
tinny tingle. What is it you crave more than
simple shelter, hay-bed in a barn? Your prayer,
where to find fields with no fence to pen you,
free to be loved by the quietest cloud.

Beech, Birch, Buckthorn

What breaks the heart more than autumn,
yellow leaves fallen fragile as a child's
grasp of joy. The porcelain doll dropped,
broken, and then the cry, as if to startle
God. A letter reads, *Who will never abandon*
whomever you thought you were? No one.
You who liked pretty colors and never looked
at the texture of trunk, the roots gripping, sunken.
But the way leaves catch in wet wind, blur
of rain, motion of water through air, water
ending without ending, how the heart hears.
Breathe in and everyone breathes. Breathe out,
the world exhales. Only the child, fevered, could know:
Not to pray, not even for nothing, but to become prayer.

This Shade Won't Ink Why You Are Shy

God presses from your soul sweet attar
or beads your body to paste-rolled rosary.
But you plead: no cross but a tree in the whole,
what can't clothe the hill, clouds of unwanted
angelica: invaders. Their spindly parts look purple.
He tells you a secret to mime the taste of grapes,
*You can go home now. The house burnt by voices
is safe.* Says bruises hide how love breaks.
Like a child who sees how faces go vein-hot
with red in church glass, you build whispers in
his tousled hair, undo his beard with pokeberries.

Never Disparage a Moon-Girl, 1

The other girls don't understand,
won't hear rain downrushing hemlocks,
birthing crocuses from mud. Their never-
forced-to-dig hands are not callused
like yours. They laugh at how you lick
ants off daffodils to spare a day more
of glow, giggle when you count backward
to the first butterfly, forward to the last frost,
days lost nimbly but numbly. How dumb
can you be? Not to stammer with them
the names of all the boys, but to bend
beneath the first apple buds, mourning
a last glimpse of moon's white,
cradled in a drop of condensation,
how earth cries—

Promise You Will Never Go Away

Not the best. Not you are living
as best you can. That might imply
midnights fanciful as candied figs,
silk shantung. What you mean most
is muslin, something luxurious become
commonplace. So you say not the best
but the way. *I am living the only way
I can.* Nights in a makeshift box
whose roof leans, looking at the moon.
Scraping pinto beans from a broken tin.
But it's here, isn't it, *here:* the best
you can do, seven coins, while
what's white sifts as if shorn—
little lamb of the air, little star.

Never Disparage a Moon-Girl, 2

Cheeks blush, as though dawn sunders a body.
Such shame, shame, to be ragged, to be rent, to be
unceasingly the seed of all-and-ever's contumely,
not comely in costume but a calamity of form
once-over-uglied from their scorn. Those girls
who eye you in wait, clamor their magpie-shrill
calls to bait your only beauty, your one soft-
spoken sentence: *Come sticks and stones, come*
talons and tricks, I will love the shy dove inside us.

A Respite from the Ice

Just now, you remember. From
white dogwoods shadowing shallow
lake-edge, lifted like what knows no bones
to float, rooted otherwise where a chipmunk
skitters up trunk, all eye on you, all eye.
Everything is looking. Through you.
Because there is nothing, in this moment,
else. Everything is saying the underside of
the names you know and do not, saying how
you, too, are alive, with nothing to gain but
your diminishment. Fiddleheads unfurled into ferns,
scraping a music without wind. For a moment,
for a fraction of a moment, no winter. Just now,
in your bones, in the ash of your bones, no winter.

Colder the Arriving than What Arrives

Much easier is glue than the horse's hooves,
kicking death to powder. Today snow falls
on the ravaged pines, half-sawed and half-seen
in a blur that can't hold but by moments—
nothing to hold except the holding itself, thin
wind warping your hands red—how they grip
and would grasp forever this lastness of frost,
something to trust before love melts everything.
What makes thaw one more weather? Emptiness
enters your body more chill than forgetting,
no way to know where the grieved go now
or if there is a land purer than violets, than silence.

Lonely the Lake, and Sere the Sedges

November unraveling a skein of sky:
wounded cries of geese fly low over a day
moon. Juxtapose yarn with tasseled tufts
of bulrushes. Juxtapose fleece with what
happens when a child's not trusted to ripple
water with rocks, disturb a peace already
in eddies from a guileless, creaturely wind—
invisible we are told, except in its hassle
of leaves, its rattle of cattails. But the child
knows wind is other than touch, and gives in
to beams of other-glow. Circles of sadness
widen in the wake of refusal. We all hope
the wind will hold us—someday—carefully,
when we are born to the half-here sky.

No Tomorrows

It ached you, to know it would
and wouldn't always stay, no telling
what but how the lake opened, angled
inside to a border of blackening hillocks,
hedge crickets keening this moment without
form—and before, how a coffin built
your body to a box you couldn't beyond—
but now this expanse, horizoned below
and above in mauves, pale pinks. Vees
of geese veering, not again seen or before,
as windows into wakes of wordlessness
omen no tomorrows, only a voice sole, singing:
Just stand here. And know this as your worth.

In the Red Night Clouds

If you paint the heavens red, some moon
will arise, bobbing to the surface like a toy,
a boy's lost ball buoyed up, contending
with red water and red fish who breathe red.
Look at the moon and it changes; shadows
curved against such bright light can't but give
back your best and worst dreams, torqued
to a strangeness, a disguise, that hides all
you're not ready to see. Look at anything long
and it will beat in the pulse of your blood: a bird
navigating the night, owl with its heart face,
the berry bushes of your garden mouthing *hush*.
Look longer still and all dissolves: one color,
one moon, all earth, red as love, red as living.

If Wings Neither Waxed nor Waned

Death rattles your name in its throat. If your
clawfoot bathtub is full of captured pigeons,
your hair knots from sheer lack of rain. Pull
pain up the spiral staircase, take down fringed,
frayed shawls from the wardrobe's dim musk.
Death dreads not dust on a mirror—*Polish it,
polish it, not one speck should show*—Death whets
its tooth when you look in shallows and see
depths, no mirror, no eyes with a child's sad wisdom,
losing a game. The more you abide in the body,
the more your body is not. Death hears pigeons
coaxing, cooing, a cough like last, labored breath.
*My doves, what are we? Cloak of the moon and bone-
winds of stars. And light—we know not from aught.*

IV

All my joy

If grace were a toy. If God were a boy and his cradle a blue top, spinning. Blue, oh blue, over all, under. I'd pray trade the doll in her frown. I'd pray trade these blooms—pluck and wither, pluck and wither, twine, twine, woodbine, fennel, trumpet-tunnel. Take crow-flowers, take nettles, take salt. Weave me a dress not of daisies. If God were something small and encauled, I'd count a coil to high clouds' rocking. I thought I could make myself something more than a stone, but the church had already its rock. And said I should bend, slim tree when wind makes a slim wish through it. And said I should sing, as robins bleed pleasant to sky. So the willow down-follows my fancy. How poor is a pebble, a purple. Float me, blue-shimmered on sun-cut water. See this bubble? Here and then not. Oh here, oh here—stay, bubble, stay bubble, stay bubble, stay—

Notes

"All of It Alive": The phrase "This fleeting world" is borrowed from *The Diamond Sutra.*

"Of the Notebook's Eyes" borrows some facts from the life of Unica Zürn, the German writer and artist who took her life by defenestration.

"Moon-Girls of the Burning Barn" finds its source in the "Parable of the Burning House" in *The Lotus Sutra.* The story, in my retelling, is much amended and this source may not even be recognizable as such.

"Flowers for the Executioner": The italicized sentences are from Matthew 5:44 (KJV).

"Unknowing the Clouds" takes its title and some of its content from *The Cloud of Unknowing,* a religious treatise written in Middle English by an unknown fourteenth-century mystic.

"Unwriting the Sentence": "Nightly, it flaps out" is borrowed from Sylvia Plath's "Elm."

"Of the Cloud In-Between" is based on a heliogravure of Gustav Klimt's *Medicine.*

"Song of Languor": The rhythms of the phrases in this poem that are not italicized attempt to follow a motif from a composition by David Gelfand, originally of this title.

Section II: The titles in particular and some of the language in these poems borrow heavily from Shakespeare's *Hamlet.* All of the titles are taken from Ophelia's lines, except "A toy in blood," which is spoken by Laertes to Ophelia.

"Moon-Girls of the Medicine" combines a meditation on the painting *Bird Medicine* by Anne Siems with the recollection of coming out of a coma.

"To Limn a Limbed Thing": The first two lines are borrowed from "Eihei Koso Hotsuganmon" or "Dogen's Vow," by Eihei Dogen.

"Never Disparage a Moon-Girl": This poem, like "Moon-Girls of the Burning Barn," finds its source in *The Lotus Sutra,* here in the "Parable of the Bodhisattva Never Disparaging."

"In the Red Night Clouds" was written in response to an untitled painting by Louis Schneider.

"If Wings Neither Waxed nor Waned": What is said about the mirror in this poem borrows its source from *The Platform Sutra.*

Acknowledgments

Heartfelt thanks to the editors of the journals where these poems first appeared, often in earlier versions:

The *Adroit Journal:* "A Matryoshka Doll Is a Nest Made of Eggs" (as "Because a Matryoshka Doll Is a Nest Made of Eggs")

Bone Bouquet: "Of the Light Before Darkness" and "Of Thread and Absence" (as one poem: "Sky Thin as Thread")

The *Carolina Quarterly:* "Beech, Birch, Buckthorn" and "Here the Woods Come in Too Close" (as "Palette Unpainted in Her Thick Bark")

Cider Press Review: "Of the Notebook's Eyes" (as "Not the Notebook but Those Better Blessed")

The *Cincinnati Review:* "Of the Cloud In-Between" (as "Cloud of the In-Between")

CutBank: "In the Red Night Clouds" and "Unknowing the Clouds"

Diode: "Flowers for the Executioner," "Little Heavenling" (as "Clouds Guess the Moon's Retort") and "Silence, a Prayer of Wax" (as "Ear, Ear, Unasked")

Ecotone: "When World Is Whale"

Hermeneutic Chaos: "All of It Alive" (as "Oh, Ophelia, Why Without Wonder, When Wings") and "Death's Secrets like a Box" (as "Ophelia Finds No Fault with Folly")

The *Journal:* "Low to Ground and Listening" and "They Break Open in Sun but Stay Dark"

Linebreak: "If Wings Neither Waxed nor Waned"

Lumina: "Moon-Girls of the Burning Barn" (parts 1 and 2, as one poem)

Luna Luna: "Memory of Sin," "Of Bubbles and Milk" (as "Something Wet and Floaty and Once"), "Of Water and Echo" (as "Because Bark Is Neither Boat nor a Hearkening"), and "Unwriting the Sentence"

Moledro Magazine: "Never Disparage a Moon-Girl" (parts 1 and 2, as one poem)

New Orleans Review: all the poems in Sections II and IV were published here as a sequence titled "Ophelia"

Phoebe: "Moon-Girls of the Medicine" (as "Moon-Girls of the Medicine Birds")

Southern Indiana Review: "A Respite from the Ice" (as "A Respite from the Ice of Self-Rendering")

Stirring: "A Dream of Sea Urchins" (as "Ophelia Dreams of Sea Urchins")

Thrush Poetry Journal: "Song of Languor"

Tupelo Quarterly: "Faint Stars of Dread" and "To Limn a Limbed Thing"

The *Westchester Review:* "Portrait of a Storm" (as "Storm")

"A Matryoshka Doll Is a Nest Made of Eggs" was reprinted in *The Doll Collection* (Terrapin Books, 2016) under its original title.

"Beech, Birch, Buckthorn" and "When World Is Whale" were reprinted in *Moledro Magazine*.

Some of the poems from this manuscript appeared in chapbooks. All twelve poems from Sections II and IV were printed in *Ophelia* (dancing girl press, 2016), though in earlier versions. The poems "Of the Cloud In-Between," "In the Red Night Clouds" and "Unknowing the Clouds" were included in *Spirits of the Humid Cloud* (dancing girl press, 2012).

* * *

Deepest gratitude to John Yau for selecting my manuscript as the winner of the 2018 Colorado Prize for Poetry: I don't know how to thank you enough.

Also, true and abiding thanks to Stephanie G'Schwind of the Center for Literary Publishing at Colorado State University and all the staff of both the Center and the University Press of Colorado: without your generous efforts this book wouldn't be in the world.

Thank you to all the kind people, friends and editors, who took time with this manuscript and helped me to see the weaknesses of earlier drafts. Nan Becker, Cynthia Cruz, Ellen Devlin, Jennifer Franklin, Kate Knapp Johnson, Maggie Smith, and Lynn Schmeidler, I owe you a great debt for your wise comments and your gentle hearts.

Thank you to all my writing comrades in the Thursday night poetry group. I am grateful for our companionship in the world of words.

Thank you, sincerely, to my new therapist, my new Zen teacher, and my nutritionist/herbalist for getting me through hard times. And to my friends, who give me a reason.

Love to my mom, my stepfather, and my mother-in-law.

And lastly, thank you, as always, to Rich, for that which is immeasurable and beyond my comprehension. You help me to see God in all things.

Thank you to God. Or to Buddha, Dharma, and Sangha.

This book is set in Sabon
by the Center for Literary Publishing
at Colorado State University.

Copyediting by Daniel Schonning.
Proofreading by Kristin Macintyre.
Book design and typesetting by Michelle LaCrosse.
Cover design by Stephanie G'Schwind.
Cover photo by Brooke Shaden.
Printing by BookMobile.